Where The BAEDEKER LEADS

A Poetic Journey

JAMES YEKU

MAWENZI
HOUSE

We acknowledge the support of the Canada Council for the Arts for our publishing program. We also acknowledge support from the Government of Ontario through the Ontario Arts Council, and the support of the Government of Canada through the Canada Book Fund.

ONTARIO ARTS COUNCIL
CONSEIL DES ARTS DE L'ONTARIO
an Ontario government agency
un organisme du gouvernement de l'Ontario

Canada Council for the Arts Conseil des arts du Canada

Canada

Cover design by Babatunde Idowu-Taylor
Cover photo credit: Pietro De Grandi

Library and Archives Canada Cataloguing in Publication

Title: Where the Baedeker Leads / James Yékú.
Names: Yeku, James, author.
Description: Poems.
Identifiers: Canadiana (print) 20210245662 | Canadiana (ebook) 20210245719 | ISBN 9781774150504 (softcover) | ISBN 9781774150511 (EPUB) | ISBN 9781774150528 (PDF)
Classification: LCC PS8647.E49 W54 2021 | DDC C811/.6—dc23

Printed and bound in Canada by Coach House Printing

Mawenzi House Publishers Ltd.
39 Woburn Avenue (B)
Toronto, Ontario M5M 1K5
Canada
www.mawenzihouse.com

The voice that speaks as the sound of many waters,
uttering words that burn with energy. Words
that roar as thunder into the Sun's eternity.

Also, Kemi:
for furious love that sets us on a queendom's sail
yet prodding back to Eden's harbor.

CONTENTS

II

III

FOREWORD

Òrìsà oríta reclaims his stories

Nduka Otiono
Institute of Africa Studies, Carleton University, Canada

As we approach the end of the first quarter of the twenty-first century and the end of the International Decade for People of African Descent (2015–2024), the quantity and character of literary works by new African diaspora writers increasingly call for attention outside of the circumscribed disciplinary spaces of African Studies or Postcolonial Studies. Besides the growing number of publications and the impressive quality of some of the works by a new generation of African immigrant writers, the Black Lives Matter and post-George Floyd anti-Black racism consciousness has kindled an expanded literary sensibility that now accommodates newer voices that were previously overlooked and rendered invisible by the politics of canonization.

By "new African diaspora" immigrants I mean Africans who since the last decade of the twentieth century voluntarily relocated to North America and who are probably more in number than those whose ancestors were trafficked as slaves in the nineteenth century. It is important to further clarify that, although the focus in this foreword is on new African diaspora immigrants in Canada and the United States, the reference extends to an understanding of the term diaspora as representing "a global space, a worldwide web, that accounts as much for the mother continent as for wherever in the world her offspring may have been driven by the unkind forces of history," to borrow from the scholar and novelist Isidore Okpewho in his introduction to the volume *The New African Diaspora* (1999).

Among the new African diaspora immigrants is Nigerian-born, Canadian-trained and U.S.-based academic and poet, James Yeku. His debut collection of poems Where the Baedeker Leads not only opens an additional window for viewing this new millennium immigrant experience, but also reminds us of a salient declaration by the the literary sage Chinua Achebe in his simple yet magisterial essay, "What has literature got to do with it" published in *Hopes and Impediments* (1989). As Achebe writes, "It is in the very nature of creativity, in its prodigious complexity and richness, that it will accommodate paradoxes and ambiguities" (110). Indeed, in this collection, Yeku presents the reader a panoply of the rich, complex, paradoxical, and ambiguous experiences with which the new African diaspora immigrant—sometimes referred to as the Afropolitan—grapples. To deal with this broad range of experiences, Yeku adopts a journey motif that is tied to the title of the collection, *Where the Baedeker Leads*. The key word in the title, "Baedeker," from the print tradition of travel guidebooks produced and popularized by the German publisher Karl Baedeker, invites the reader to partake in the poet-persona's spatial, temporal, and psychological pilgrimage.

The opening poem introduces the initial locale—the prairie city Saskatoon, described by the poet as "The city that adorns bridges, Paris / of the Prairies, rightly named" (1). The poet then unfolds the complexity of his experience as he transcends the geographic space or physicality of the cityscape to apprehend the human and psychological complement of the experience. He moves beyond the city streets to recognize that "Saskatoon is its people, / radiant souls tipsy with dreams / and dreaming gently / in the conical comforts of Indian tipis" (1). However, the poem ends with a startling twist that highlights the isolation of the poet-persona. For against the backdrop of the wintry flurries, the promise of warmth and companionship offered by a bird which welcomes the speaker's gaze, disappears. In response to the poet-persona's opening of his window to let the bird in "to share [his] space and loneliness" (2), the bird "refuses, preferring the cold outside / to the oven of [his] condo" (Ibid.). Upon which, the poet-persona looks "away, stung by her rejection" (Ibid.).

This first poem at once becomes a synecdoche of the immigrant experience that the poet-persona explores in this collection. Divided into three uneven sections—with the first section having the greatest number of poems—*Where the Baedeker Leads* portrays the poet-persona's imaginary return from the diaspora to his homeland. Soon after we witness him dealing with life in wintry Saskatoon in the opening poem, together with the oppressive pandemic lockdown isolation which "sucked life out of us, / like a raisin that grows dour in the mouth" in the poem "Isolation" (3-4), the troubadour cycles across various places including Chicago, Angola prison in Louisiana, and Lagos. Although the poet notes that "Poetry is born, so is the union / of strange tales and tongues" (7), the proclamation that the Baedeker leads to "this doorway to arcane futures" (7) appears not only deceptive but seemingly intended not to be read literally.

The bulk of the poems in the first and second sections traverse broad experiences that include racial ("Take a Knee," 18) and everyday social and political experiences in the diaspora and in the African homeland where we witness "Masters of corruption's nipples, / ...spray fetid Naira notes / on the ornamented heads / of Owambe belles" (13). In focusing attention on the devaluing of the Nigerian currency—the Naira—and by extension, the corruption of the economy by "Lords of the commonwealth" (13) and "Prophets, drunk with earthly power" (Ibid), Yékú provides justification for the popular Nigerian youth rebellion of October 2020 called the #endSARS uprising. As the poet observes,

> Like a tree that falls, the Nigerian human
> is a forest that crumbles and nothing makes a sound.
> Until now, as the cry against despots
> ricochets in gestures to #endSARS. (19)

The spotlight on the well-coordinated social movement against police brutality via the #endSARS protests enables the poet to engage in a veiled ridicule of the political leadership in the homeland ("Bubu," 30 and "Field of Dreams," 24-25, and "Sai Baba," 29-31).

The poet's identification with the plight of the Nigerian youth who represent the future of the country and his scholarly interest as a Digital Humanities scholar are manifest in several poems that foreground the promises and limits of digital media, including another "hashtag poem," #BringBackOurGirls (35-36). Here, the poet revisits the April 2014 tragic abduction of about 276 young girls from their school in Chibok in northeastern Nigeria by Boko Haram terrorists. The two-stanza poem ends with touching tender lines that set the tone for the "love" poems in the mid-second section which bridges this first and the third sections of the collection: "You too are my sister, though you know neither me / Nor the many lights combing Sambisa for you" (26).

In poems such as "I Feel Like Dreaming About You Tonight" (54), "these heartstrings" (55), "To hold and not have" (57), "Adúmáradán" (62) and "This night is ours" (63) the poet offers us some relief from the aches and stresses of the opening section. Here the poet-persona allows himself the luxury of sensual liaisons to prepare him for the final, plaintive section. From lines such as "I feel like dreaming about you tonight. / Will you allow your tenderness to ripen in my desires" (54) in the early part of section two, the poet tapers off this section with an invocation of the trickster archetype in the closing lines of "This night is ours" (63):

Tonight, soft desires will stroke
the silky slopes of loins
and Èsù's erect man
will smile at us. (63)

Such carefree sensuality in section two hardens into the mournful tone of the final section which ricochets with elements of oral tradition introduced by the allusion to Èsù, the trickster god in the Yoruba pantheon. The departed people celebrated by the poet in this section are Pius Adesanmi, the Nigerian Canadian writer, professor, and former Director of the Institute of African Studies at Carleton University who died in the Ethiopian Airline crash of March 10, 2019 ("Wayfarer," 72-73); Harry Garuba, poet and professor of English at University of Cape Town who died on February 28, 2020 ("Death of an Unharried Poem," 74); and Chinua Achebe and Nelson Mandela—also known as Madiba ("Ancestors," 77-78). These memorial poems segue into the closing poems of the book which return us to the travel motif in the poem "Lord of the Crossroads" (79), while reclaiming oral traditional elements that highlight the poet's understanding of African oral aesthetics.

Hence, in the last three poems—"Lord of the Crossroads" (79), Mother Earth (80), and Móremí (81-82)—Yeku robustly embraces his Yoruba cultural roots. Besides promoting the rich mythopoeic worldview of his people, which is also popular in the Americas, he adopts the griot's bardic voice to celebrate the legendary "princess of Ife" (82) and heroine of the Yoruba nation, Queen Móremí, who delivered the land from the stranglehold of "a two-eyed terror [who] ruled the earth from the underworlds of Ife." (Ibid.)

In the end, the new African diaspora immigrant and poet-persona closes with a homecoming. He successfully bridges or hyphenates the two worlds to which he now belongs—the diaspora and the homeland. He is like the "òrìsà oríta, reclaiming [his] stories" (79). Significantly, in this line, the poet-persona, as the mythic Èsù himself, contests hegemonic misrepresentations of Yoruba narratives of spirituality by reclaiming a space of self-enunciation. Since the colonial demonization of Èsù—erroneously rendered as Satan in cultural discourses—persists, there is a sense in which we may argue that the so-called arbiters of Yoruba culture and mythologies have not effectively upset such troubling perspectives; hence, the trickster-god himself emerges poetically in the light of his linguistic abilities as the judge of his own discursive fate, transgressive in his insistence on setting the records straight.

Beyond the longing for a distant home and the cuddles of strangers in a foreign land, then, James Yeku's debut poetry book sucks the reader into the apparitions that every sensitive troubadour in exile confronts, while offering meditations on the psycho-social experiences and impulses they endure. Between these pages, "poetry is born" as "the union / of strange tales and tongues," to paraphrase the poet-persona. *Where the Baedeker Leads* is a commendable collection, especially for those at the crossroads of life.

WORKS CITED

Achebe, Chinua. *Hopes and Impediments: Selected Essays.* New York: Doubleday, 1989.

Okpewho, Isidore, Carole B. Davies and Ali A. Mazrui. Eds. *The New African Diaspora*. Bloomington: Indiana University Press. 1999.

I

Saskatoon

1

The city that adorns bridges, Paris
of the Prairies, rightly named.
Starry smiles embellish the midnight sky,
serenading the gaze; splendor,
the maiden's grace.
Broadway's magic spreads
like fragrance along the
jazzy waves of laughter;
riversides drenched
in sunniest rays
bestriding pathways,
leading to downtown and 8th.
A cacophony of buzzing cafes
and coming winds call out your name;
their majesty, trailing you home;
and the South River, where
bends and dreams straddle,
then merge into a frozen beauty,
or into extended snowy nights
of shared aloneness.
Saskatoon is its people,
radiant souls tipsy with dreams,
dreaming gently
in the conical comforts of Indian tipis.
Get on its brass-colored bridges
and cross into life

2

Again, the snow descends as it always does in Saskatoon,
soft and rapid, like angry waterfall scattered to earth.
I survey the vastness of mist
by my window, an oasis of lushness,
covered by whiteness and stories.

A bird welcomes my gaze,
flapping spectacle and melodies,
minding not the wintry flurries,
the regalia of tired feathers. More snow,
as I think of the poor creature—unable
to find heat or shelter in the safety of the wild.
Wings flap out her desires, looking for warmth
in the cold of trees that whisper together
in frigid voices.

I open my window to let her in,
to share my space and loneliness,
but she refuses, preferring the cold outside
to the oven of my condo.
I look away, stung by her rejection,
piqued by an avine pride I cannot fathom.

Isolation

The lockdown woke up with a tepid sun,
dragging a lifetime of grief with it.
It was an Island without stories or lilies
to flaunt fragrances of blooms, or
streams sparkling with sunshine.

Only dirges to the empty chair
at the evening meal of mandrakes.
The years before joust for infamy,
sashaying sideways poppies
from thawing clay that drips
with the warmth of an infected summer.

The Isolation sucked life out of us,
like a raisin that grows dour in the mouth.
Until strangers became lovers,
And a cache of losses sprang
into a sycamore.

But imagine you can be with friends
face to face again, without a mute bottom
standing between you, without the dread
of times, dull and quiet because
of an unwanted fever to the earth.

Imagine the year sunshine can stand
on your shoulder again, as breeze blows
kids to playground and trees sway
gleefully to welcome you to the woods.

Imagine the sights of cities
full of tourists again, the bustles
of crowds and colours uniting
into a poem of marble, places where
the collusion of minarets and crosses,
thistles and roses, is preferred to
the isolation that suffocates.

Imagine what was not normal,
but a fact of existence becoming
the greatest longing of the soul.

Transition

The suddenness of change beckons from prairie
to prairie, aspirations dissolving
again into a verdant flatness, as maize stalks
stand surreally in unformed solidarity,
popping corn after the fragrance of harvest.

Arrival is the home of a poet,
despised and beloved,
who emblazons Lawrence's hills with pride.
On Mount Oread, the stars above tell tales of freedom,
beaming from wondrous heights
upon the faces of farmers and fighters.

There, repose is vouchsafed you by fate,
after grumbling adios
to lovers and friends to the north of the borders.

And on reunion's morning, under the wintry skies
of Saskatoon's shines, we will remember
the cuddles of strangers and the guttural groans
of elders bidding us welcome again
without guns to their heads.

The Artist

after Wendell Berry

Once there was a man who filmed his existence.
He went collecting his stories in selfies,
with a smartphone to his fingers, making
a gallery of the finest images life brought him,
of the places and faces his clicks could find
in the busy and fleeting world around him. His records
preserved his body, freezing it forever: its gait and graces,
and blingy necklaces. The forced smiles of a skillful artist
holding a selfie stick to capture on camera
the many seasons of the life he was having,
so that he may document for himself
the passing moments of today in a selfie
he may never have in the future. With hands
swirling photos on tablet screens,
there he will be, staring at himself
in times gained but lost: there he will be,
even if he doesn't recognize himself.

Traveler

Here, right in these daydreams
of dithering rhymes and rhythms
wherein metaphors scurry out
to witness the kisses of parted hearts,

a poet is not to be trusted with words.
Delicate as the perching of a half-moon
upon sly and seductive skies
are the incantations of his artful epithets.

He labors through soulish labyrinths,
as a hero questing for an unknown self;
the pilgrimage of the seeking warrior
ends at these crossroads of language.

Poetry is born, so is the union
of strange tales and tongues. Here
is where the Baedeker leads:
this doorway to arcane futures.

Away from Lagos

What life is there but comings and goings?
Every city was once a paradise
in which you played the part.
Like Lagos, a city of inchoate dreams dithering
aimlessly until they are born
as a dawn without clouds.

Its harmattan is unlike the fury of winter,
but it kisses the skin with fierceness,
as blowing winds gather dust, and plaster
the face with the dryness of wet dew
and the misery of happy strangers.
The Sahara always visits again,
bearing boastful tales of angry cold
upon travelers evading a deluge of rain
drumming wildly on rusted roofs.

But Lagos keeps swaying triumphantly,
dancing as a city that breaks
the twilight grey of dusk and explodes
into a patch of colors and traffic. A city
overflows with beautiful chaos, ecstatic
its lagoon, detached from the Atlantic
that calls you away.

Beyond desires that desiccate and rotten,
beyond daydreams that drift into reality,
here lies a city whose inhabitants embrace

from afar, preferring winter
to the smell and thrills of home.

And after crossing the river,
you were sure the ice crystals of snow
would shine a light on the night
that welcomed you.

To be rescued
from winds roaring like harmattan's fury
was your only prayer sacred fires
from quivering lips.

But desires, unaided by sense,
melt like a candle
rushing to burn its wax.

And when you look back
to the home you left,
it recedes into shadows,
a mirage that haunts like
the apparitions that made you flee.

My Chicago

That is no place to scurry past, lest you
miss twittering birds rivaling tourists for podiums,
dancing flowers swaying coyness to spring rains,
or a carnival of faces, busy and flooding cities
with radiating friendliness and quaint little smiles.
Lake Michigan is my witness, there nature's artifice
is perfected, to trick owners too proud to behold beauty
away from awesome bustles,
to tickle weary travelers
to seductive waves and skylines.
And life is cooler by its waters,
and windy too, the turns of events
and of roaring trains, Metra, pacing TAs and profs
around universities and shopping malls.
A caravan of skyscrapers, too, adorn busy streets
with a foreplay of splendor,
promising pleasuring sights at nights,
at Downtown and Loops.
Gorgeous sunny days we had,
and plenty of dreams to dream, yet very few words
to scribble what startled most:
the wide-eyed lakefronts, or the millennium magic,
and the Chicago mix
of watery sandwiches
that remain in your mouth
back home
in your own city.

The Student

The fire burns in her heart,
as flames kindled by the sagely
coercions of youth.

Not the wisest of teachers
could tame the genie
bottled in a sweet soul,
of candled lights and candor.

As serene waters to the restless,
the fountains form within
sang tranquilities to his battles.

Earth is his reward,
the student is master of the aged.
An afterlife of giftings
breaking before them on earth.

She was born before her time
a golden mind, the guardian of gazes
and peers to brightening blossoms.

On the Cusp of Conquest

Not here, nor there still. Liminal,
father's dreams breaking into mine,
merging memories and kismets
in kisses of promises fulfilled.

Aged eyes will search for wetness
to ferry ululations across the Atlantic,
finding light in the dimness that once engulfed.

This threshold, ripped and ripened anon,
shall meet father's embrace
at the end of sprouted paths taken.

In victories denied ancestors gone by time,
a father's beau sparkles in effulgence;
His *geste*, a hero's conquest
beyond the great river.

Prebendal Blues

That is no sleaze which begets legal thievery.
Slashing a nation in whirring frenzies,
an emblem of troubled soul is a clangor
of arguments.

Our kerfuffle is chaos,
resting in the potbellies of prebends,
Lords of the commonwealth, cajoling
the passionless to no end.
They are the men of puissance,
ogling China's march across the land
with hostile adoration.
Masters of corruption's nipples,
they spray fetid Naira notes
on the ornamented heads
of *Owambe* belles.

To satiate the unceasing bleats of avarice,
they beshrew the oily coffers
and pray curses on the putrid fingers
of prophecy. Prophets, drunk with earthly power,
break out in the unknown tongues of Lakshmi.
The gyres of their communion erect
a pyre of truth, its ashes floating beyond the Niger.

Shadows

Hurray to shadows that steal
into your dawn like an apparition
on a grey sky,

the face of heaven
mourning the tares of fears

till, at last, the sequins
drift back into your eyes,

with glows that shame
jagged silhouettes.

In difference

What now for throats
slit in the throes of ugly nights
too familiar for mourning?

Lamentation, the requiem of earth
leaning towards a bloodied moon
rising again upon the hasty prayers
of these felled by terror,

brothers wrapped in the shroud
of our indifference.

The clothes of memories

are in Angola to welcome you. Again.
So do mean-looking sergeants
strolling like a mother with children full of pranks.
Yet you crave for their attention as crack,
for survival.

What must be done
to never walk back here? Desolate longings
that paralyze you, interrogating without mercy.
You plead for dignity,
but the high-barbed wires around block your prayers
from ascending to realms, Elysian,

their voices torment you
like a bird caged to stalking silence by
a fistful of fears. They dance in your head
like millennials dreaming dangerous dreams
with feet and selfies
on crowded dancing floors.

You dream of the 'hood and the boys,
and then you realize there ain't no brother
behind bars, only the guy who
always introduces himself to everyone:
"Hello, my name is Trouble."

You retreat to yourself as before,
finding company in solitude and sometimes

in half-baked verses like these ones
describing a beleaguered journey in orange land.

And then you step out
into your gated community,
only to find you are back at home:
you are free, but for a moment.
"32469!" There is a warder yelling a code.

Take a Knee

The art of being black when all lives matter
Is no art at all, only inchoate rhymes demanded
by alter egos and unloving allies.

Through the seasons of our lives, our knees
have bended to the wishes of blazing guns,
            choking smokes
from firearms in the blue hands
            of law-abiding ogres.

Heralding an avalanche
of rocks and bottles, they scoff at US
for kneeling but march to kneel their rage
on the neck of Justice.

A clash of bended knees and occupied breathing
stumble against one another,
the flames of fury whitewashed into silence.
Struggling, the soul bestriding realms,
succumbs to stillness, eternal.

But we bend the knees again, chanting
what matter in Blues of protest,
to reclaim beautiful bodies and stories
from a broken country.

#endSARS

The Nigerian human, like a tree that falls
in an uninhabitable forest, is never heard.
Not by potbellied prebends whose noses
perceive only the smelly melodies
of their own ramblings.

Not by monsters whose belch is a tirade
hurling loud boastings after a conquest
of the communion table.

Not by the gunshots of generals tongue-tied
by the horrors of consciences seared
by the ugliness of indifference.

Like a tree that falls, unheard and unsung,
the Nigerian human is an echo of silences
misperceived into oblivion by the absence of those
for whom it sings.

Like a tree that falls, the Nigerian human
is a forest that crumbles and nothing makes a sound.
Until now, as the cry against despots
ricochets in gestures to #endSARS.

Bubu

The streets are heaving with anxieties,
as screens and smartphones pour tales of griefs
into your chest; you wonder what gestures
to end czars will unloose the tongue of Bubu.

But alas, Bubu speaks, but of clouds without rain,
dreaming hurricanes as he gaslights a nation
without fuel, in a paradise drained of life and luster;
those who die are as the cattle of Daura, invisible.

Simulacrum

A hug or a kiss
on a BlackBerry's screen
is nothing but
a torture to a soul
in need of nurture;

this winter shall
likewise embrace your skin,
its chill and winds
to sing sonnets
to the choruses
of a dream reclaimed.

The distance that
separates two hearts
is now nothing
but a melting ice of tears—
tears that comfort
at the sight of every selfie
sent by the hands
of sympathetic airwaves.

We are no more shadows
that kiss the air
or who embrace totems of
smiley memories,
neither are we specters
that Skype up

presences you are unable
to hold or cuddle.

The sea that divides
us dries up today,
not as a tale of
passionate graphics. But as
a season unwrapped
by gentle reality.

Can you see the mist
clearing, and here too,
the vapor vanishing?

This media face
is a crowded place,
the virtual assembly
of caring but
intruding witnesses.

So let us return
to the ground
where dances are meant
for us two,

where messages are shared
in the coven of
friendly mothers,

where a virgin wall
invites the scribbles
of a revived muse.

Between you and me,
lost in this legend
beneath the waist,

let us reclaim our space
offline.

Field of Dreams

In the field of dreams
we gather hopes,
staring storms into hiding
and sashaying ourselves
with promises
of summer's
coming shines
that sway and twinkle
like stars.

We gather guts too,
servants and peasants,
singing victory songs
with the wild melodies
of untiring blizzards.

Dark-goggled despots
mock our dance,
singing tales of
afterlives of shadows
and dreams deferred.

But the field falls, its roses
fading, yet ripe with promises
of healing and love.

And the field feels like home too,
calling us to return to

the smell of acceptance
and a flurry of flowers dancing to revive
the faint figures of the struggle.

Hot Spot

1

I am bound to this land by bytes,
my vision strained by its screen.
Routed through its labyrinths and streets,
its algorithms travel in my networks.
I hear the rants and raves of users
morphing guys into games and nots into bots;
I feel the weight of its wired burdens,
and I know the fantasies of its paths,
the wishes of its feeds erupt in my mind
leaving messages exploding in my head
like a mishmash of spannin' and unplugged rhythms.

I have heard the cryptic cheers of delusions
deleting truths from defragged girls.
I have seen Incels reduce its space to empires
splashing its walls with dreams of self-glories;
I have seen words bow at floodgates of faces,
faces flooding gates at 4:04 and refusing to be broken
by ancient links or rhizomes.

2

I have seen men cached out by knotty cookies,
teens taken by leery eyes trolling away lies.
I have seen images dance to the vain beats of selfies,

phonies selling cheap sex to babies,
and princes scamming thieves abroad for bread.
I have seen the profiles of a thousand friends
liking and following fiends at unknown ends.
I have seen the memes of artful madness
and the madness of artful memes,
with the artifacts of their souls on the stages of U-tube.
I have seen the tweets of their vanities retweeted
by celebrity cults worshipping influence.

If I sing not of dulcet smiles and poses
on the screens of Instagram, or sing not of the delight,
of words to the pleasures of seeking eyes and hearts,
it is because of the capillaries of capital
which also adorn this land of unlived lives.

Because I am bound to this land,
I have seen secrets of the bedroom
Tiktoking their talk to viral fame;
with eyes in languid lands,
and I too busy to surf reality,
I have yet to see IT all . . .

Life Elsewhere

Bind not yourself to that land
which bids you to empty your being
before sprouting fantasies
of triumphs.

They have no allegiance to it, whose dreams
are a nagging nightmare of home in Sheol.
Nightmares of sword-blades
piercing and menacing
like the fury of despots
slain on the thighs of Eros.

No ties to that land that binds the young,
to that land where skies darken
each time the suns of the mighty
break upon them desiring to laugh again.

With sighs mingled with an apocalypse,
they dream of homes elsewhere,
far-flung but tranquil;
where closed hearts murmur
welcome ballads to the weariness
of their journeys.

Sai Baba

1

The noose man's forbidden steps
are back at the door;
they chant change from feeble lips
to stomachs, barren and bare;
the familiar moment of hunger pangs
bow in obeisance, fermenting rumbles and ruins
like the unwanted sweetness
of home-brewed beer.
Sire, Buhari.
Seared consciences
like Ajaokuta's flickering iron
smuggle an apology
into unsuspecting hearts;
no kerosene to light up
the paths of their perfidy
nor fuel to watch
the spectacle of
Baba's Babanriga
flowing knavishly
in the theater of anomies.

2

The noose man's forbidden steps
are back at the door,

sampling them that trudge
from the empty harvest
to a daily ritual
of anguishes inveigling as smiles.

The prophets too are back
to the pillaging of pews,
youths glued to screens retreating
to the fantasies of foreign pleasures,
the headmaster, the annual ravish
of village belles lacking spirit and fight.

3

Professors will reach for the loudest voice
at the staff club, haggling on behalf
of the rest of us,
over fly-infested liquors;
some will post a message on Facebook
proposing a Sahara of ideas
for the common sense
we crave to despise.

Sai Baba, we will chant again,
sighing squalor
to the highest bidder,
and taking selfies with Abuja urchins.
Sai, Baba, nothing but the sighs
of other levels of nightmares;

nothing but the cries

of scarred silences littering farmlands
and Plateaus with ghostly dirges
of terror and tears.
And when you hear the boastings of gunshots,
it is nothing but the wishes of power
sighing on the wings of herdsmen.

Influenza

Unruly, the mobs you love to see,
who litter your screen with chaos
when your only wish is a buddy
to cuddle and fondle to no end.

They tweet Ranka dedes to influencers
and dance hallelujah to cash giveaways
that take away from them.

Morn soon returns to their rites,
rituals of painted faces 'gramming
instantly to fame and dreaming
of paradise amidst rotten tomatoes.

Ah, the fakery of existence on the virtual
streets of our fellowship, the plastic images
of their communion etched in the selfies of
hushed puppies and poppy heads.

Influencing the converted,
a splash of life athirst for Vodka
caterwauls for the mobile screen.

Baba's Child

I am Baba's child singing lullabies to deafened politicians
And calling out rhyming clichés for more lies at the podium.

I am my mother's child running errands for the winds
And calling metaphors to her contest of wits and words.

I am a Nigerian child playing in the rain that drains a future
And begging proverbs to shelter me from another night of
fears.

I am a street child, marooned to your island of desires;
Tongue-tied by the tyranny of your care
And plagued by the iron hands of schoolmasters.

I am a child seeking a tomorrow of smiles
And treading the paths of sighs,
Yet calling birdsongs to croon the dawn ahead.

I am your child;
Reaching to pluck off my moon
By the magic of your tenderness.

Again

This one more time:
the sky is drained
of loving stars,
the land besieged
by the ghosts of angry spirits.

And the rainbow we hoped for,
darkened by the threats
of uncertain thunderstorms.

Forget the sights
that call from the worn-out breasts
of bony chests, or the sighs
of untouched succulence.
The shrieks of babies are
reeds broken by your ignorance.

As last morsels compete with
a china of grief to reach dry mouths,
the morning headlines will jostle
for viral #hashtag to ferry our pains
beyond the waters.

Then the gunshots will
begin again.

#BringBackOurGirls

1

Behold the holy minds burdened with bullets
And wielding machetes and faith.

They seek virgins in the craggy forest of their rage
And bury lust and horrors in those not of age.

Drumbeats of war rise to the Mullah's call to prayer,
With ghostly dances to the vanishing voices of forced martyrs.

If good luck sees the agonies of this hellscape,
Dusk may be the promise of a belated escape.

2

But to what shall I liken your absence this night?
A mask dancing to rhythms of panic and fear?

Or a caged bird flapping tired wings in a desert storm?
A lone voice amidst an unwilling harem of dread?

Or a child thirsting
For the strength of mother's bosom?

You too are my sister, though you know neither me
Nor the many lights combing Sambisa for you.

Your trails are the paths we follow.
Your groans, the unwanted songs of freedom.

And as those cries reach out to mother,
the memories of your voice scare Pluto's arms away.

Till the forest leads me to you.

I Am a Militant

Mine is an anthem of putrefying carcasses
Set ablaze by potbellied chiefs and multinational thieves.
Mine is a sacred song of boiling *bloods*
Composed by the pulsing flares of distant oil wells.

Mine are the atrocious rhythms of pain*full* gains
Anchored by marshals of maddening vanities and vapors.
Mine is the warbling of warring desires
Moored in the venomous waters of the delta.

Mine is the militant's ditty
Of *amnestied* woos and continuous woes.
And of natural grasses and hunting gases,
And oil and its toils.

But they say
I am a militant
Singing from the poisoned creeks
Of hostage dreams…

We stood,
Watching to see
More tears trickle down
Once again from the face of the moon.

We listened,
As leaves rustled
To the boisterous call of the winds,

With sea waves dancing to angry rattling
Threatening banks and walled streets.

Yet we waited:
Every man.
Of different creeds and diverse clans,
Looking intently at the sky
Almost washed out by greenhouse gases,
Waiting patiently for the smiling arrival
Of a friend, familiar.

We stood and listened; we waited…

Volcano

See the fears scattered in their eyes
like the scrambles of an elephant in musth.

Hear their muffled voices trembling
like the quaking rocks smoldering vile and inferno.

Feel the gyrating pulsations of souls
blackened by the lavas of an untamable monster.

They are the battered of the earth:
tattered by the riffles of tyranny,
frozen to the murky claws of uncertainty.

The broken lords of the inner cities:
chained by the harrowing hands of torture,
tongue-tied by a night void of stars.

Listen with your heart,
and you will touch the suppressed groans
of a nation seated on a volcano.

The odor of their mouths

Here are they who from the broken voices
of last night's rage call us again
to another feast of fists.

Must we listen to their anthems of war
and march to rhythms of uncertain barrel sounds?
Must we muffle our sighs and bring to combat
ferocious energies of crippling appetites?

Their words are the swords that rip
flesh open like a lioness, the blighted carcass
of a straying game in Molete's jungle.

As the strewn steps of Mama Ayoka's
dance at Odo Osi hold us in
a trance of enraptured ruins,
So does the tumult of their tongues set the ballot
                    against the masses.
                With guns
        And cuffs,
With machetes
        and the watching eye of the smartphone . . .

They imprison several in caves of carnage,
Releasing them to the waiting *arms*
of a colorless rainbow.
It is another *s*-election race,
And the odor of their mouth is back again.

Sunset

I feel your pain when the agonies of night besiege your soul,
When your rites of unheard sighs begin.

Come near, feel the gentleness of my voice:
For you I will weave metaphors to gather fleeing dreams,
With endless rhymes to soothe your troubled spirit.

For you, my lips shall lisp a dazzling tale of glee,
With a swansong of affections to seduce your tenderness.

Then after this sunset, I shall ask
Who are you for whom my heart still longs?

If We Must Sing

May it be the songs of dawn
And not the ballads of forefathers whose voices
are drowned by shame.
A broken present, a forgotten yesterday,
And the children of the Nubia
Gift lands again to greed.

Hear the sounds of grenades serenading hearts
with promises of emptiness, the labors
of true heroes, mocked by a discord of virtues.

Wipe out these memories:
of sons turned knives
and refugee camps where flies are meats
that accompany dry morsels to the mouth.
Obliterate the day the new warrior
was born on Nubian soil, and let
the tunes of a new drumbeat lead us to fresh rivers.

Wipe out the night of warring shots,
of dusk and fears seizing the future
and draining innocence from soldiers too young
to nurse the violence of another.

Who will bury the horrors of Rwanda
in the thickness of darkness
And call forth the abyss
to swallow up the ghosts of Darfur?

When shall daylight seize our dusk,
Or rouse fading voices out of their slumber?
Who shall weave tales of ceasefire
and call a people to their sunrise?

Voices

Rivers of echoes drown them again at night.
In tents that speak of stench, they frighten,
Pouring a libation of voices
to break innocence to pieces.

Little ones hide in the forest of their fears,
Shutting ears to threatening drums of war,
While clinging to the dregs of saggy breasts.
They know the rattling noise of hell,
The rapid pattering of riffles.

Ricocheting firebrand like wailing nukes,
Warlords dance to the tunes of angry bullets
Scaring them like the sounds of angry waterfalls,
Descending like a swamp of bodies
from wicked mountains of unholy desires.

They are afraid to die.
Yet the voices torment them
Like a demented monster howling horror
And sending fledgling minds to terror.
Rivers of echoes will drown them again tonight,
And tomorrow's suns may surrender to dusk.

Tòkunbọ̀

Grandpa's wavery and raspy voice is
shaky in its tenor, yet covers a sea of distance
like the many rivers Tòkunbọ̀ traversed to the unknown.

"Have you seen him?"—the voice of a beleaguered father
tearing through my heart, as images
of crashing waves carry lifeless bodies
into the abyss in my vision.

Welcomed but deeply resented, they are the scorn
of the earth, the scum of places whose love
they must accept with hate.

Tòkunbọ̀'s silence was a silhouette only dimness
could fathom; the silence of the ages merging
into an aquatic void, a nothingness alive but afloat.

We waited on the waters to wash home stories
from other lands, tales of the figure that returned
only in our dreams, claimed by fantasies of a life
elsewhere and rumors of hope desired.

So, grandpa took his flight too, journeying
not by Sicily's hungry shores into
an eternity of questions.

Desert Journey

The scorching welcome of its embrace,
a Sahara of dryness and winds,
arid, blowing away the footsteps of earlier pilgrims.

There the sun radiated proudly,
burning their skin with the touch of boastful beams,
unwanted companions of sinking feet.

One of the travelers trudged wearily through sands
that shift lazily in their speed and beauty,
prying Cacti call out with prideful pokes.

Another steadied a backpack drenched as dust
blows haze and fears from miles afar,
or so it seemed.

Until the danger that lurks in their minds
finally formed before them, the veiled ones
welding guns and trafficked drugs.

The journeying duo said their last prayers
to an unknown god. But the Tuareg greeted
them with a smile.

Freedom

Freedom is knocking at my door,
bearing tales of blowing winds to ladies' skirts,
tales of soothing calm to lovers' nights.

The sound of battle cascades no more.
like the sky that spreads over everything,
freedom descends from above,
its winds at my feet.

Her voice unshackles from tyrannies
that affect most. And like
an eagle in fullest flight,
she brings clarity to the prisoner's plight.

And, here, she stands before my door,
bearing tales of blowing winds
to birds uncaged.

insurrectional

for Sola Olorunyomi

Sometimes the strings
pull you backwards
into the backwaters
of brackish lagoons.

Yet they croon Afrobeats
and offer tales of hope,
amidst a cumulus of fears,
to the shrine of our passages.

You unfurl your
heart to their voice,
finding a figure who pulls
mischief and fingers' strings:
Bàbá Iwà, teacher.
Weaver of words that charm,
professing shrewdly
as one beyond self.

From the soul
to the many seasons
of a life's graces and gyrations,
Sola Mike, solo guerilla of
Sandinista who stares
down insurgence
from Nicaragua's
mountains.

II

If All I Get

Is warmth unfurled
With grace and hues from eyes aflame,
Then we get to set fancies ablaze,
Planting passions sweetly again.
My heart shall faint with naughtiness,
With you and me in love's true nest,
Poaching posies with fragrant smiles,
Ready to dream till any miles.
Most beautiful and dear of all,
Follow your dreams and I, your friend,
To be with you and buoy your sail,
As we drink our loves till all shall end.
And when in preps for pearly gates
With trumps of home and light so great,
With you, I will fly, with you to find
Our love himself, the Lamb that binds.

I Feel Like Dreaming About You Tonight

I feel like dreaming about you tonight.
Will you come to me like the rustlings of leaves
Or amble in like an evening sun?
Will your eyes glimmer like the stars at the sight of me
Or will your heart race to the harmonies of *soulish* songs?

I feel like dreaming about you tonight.
Will you allow your tenderness to ripen in my desires
Or rip open my flames of innocence?
Will you reach out to my warm hands of burning magic
Or simply take in the hues and marvels of my presence?

I feel like dreaming about you.
Will you allow me into the softness of your arms
Or usher me into the loftiness of your magic?

Will you sleep tonight?

these heartstrings

are a symphony
of rhymes.

Romeo
blushing at
the rainbow we paint
on tender skies,

Juliet at
the magic that surpasses
memories of night songs
from the balcony of dreams;

behold, gentle steps
trudging to the holy city
of the honeycomb.

this night,
desires too shall dance
to these bass strings
playing chords
of coyness
to delight a weary lover.

Like I have never seen the sky

Before, starry and clear
like the sparkles of Venus
in an orbit of diamonds.

I am not afraid to love,
to wrap muscular arms
around the waist of passions,
around the dreams we share.
And retweet after
every forgiven excuse.

Fall not asleep on me;
for tonight is a season of ejaculated cravings.
Tomorrow, the arrival of flowered fancies.

We'll craft the reality of yesterday's promises
into a mosaic of beautiful things, with
the canvas of tender hearts painted
like the resplendence of peacock feathers.

To hold and not have

To hold and not have;
the crevices that haunt the heart longing.
For you, forlorn and torn apart, but belonging forever.
A pastiche of voices cackles like the sound of many waters
and the playground squabbles of the littluns.

Each laughter adorns memories
that break you into my spirit,
into a hankering soul
seeking a home in the coldness
of distant prairies.

To hold and not have:
the disappearance of your presence
into the melancholy of unwanted mirth,
welling and swelling emptiness
that return visions of home to unblinking eyes.
The cravings of lustful scenes, palpable;
desire, dense and dreamy, smiling
at itself in the broken mirror
past and faded thrills require.

Each ecstasy, an embassy of silliness;
fondness and fondled bodies
receding into a faded night.
Yet I do not ignore you,
though memories forsake me.
And I will hold on still,
though I cannot have you.

Crossroads

I rode with the winds into her heart,
passion caressing my sail
like a drunk lover
staggering at the sight of wine.

Pleasures grow wings,
pounding hearts taken by rapture;
a mountain is climbed. Silence.
We lay side by side with Èsù,
swooning at the crossroads
that merge
            in his phallic dreams;
the hushes of the nights,
like the sultriness of her voice,
whisper our names: Hail, flâneurs,
in the cities of mingling limbs.

Ojú lọ̀rọ̀ wà—the face of discourse

An Ode to the smartphones that stole our heart
and leave us with silhouettes and lees as love.
When we do let them down and bid them depart,
don't we find pockets of pleasure in snuggles?

It is in your face my words seek their home:
Ojú lọ̀rọ̀ wà, not on social smokescreens—
where a selfie is king, and its stage, the world.
Those smiles still inspire any miles for you.

So, come near, and we will paint dreams
on unseen skies, lustful strokes canvassing
undulations to unthinkable realms.

Let us speak as in time past,
the scented cantos of perpetual nights.
Let us comfort ourselves with summer solace
and chirp kisses to the budded flowers of affections.
Ojú lọ̀rọ̀ wà: your eyes, the domicile of my verses.

Your face frees my words to fly,
like an eagle's ascent and the summits
of singing lovebirds in a gossamer of pleasures.

Ojú lọ̀rọ̀ wà: your face, not these screens
that steal, is the abode of discourse.

Starry

The Elysian graces of her poses
compare only to the virtues of roses.

The gems of her cheeks, like sequins, sparkle
as young stars from a sky of marbles.

We will melt into each other,
whispering tales that linger into eternity,

drawing out the memories of dreams
into an effulging rainbow of realness.

We will be woven into a tapestry of love,
draped in the colours of the Sun in sacred radiance.

Our heartbeats shall be a communion of laughter,
every bone, a prayer for blooms, brighter . . .

So, we will play by the rivers of affections,
and there meditate on the secrets of grasslands.

We will worship on the altar of desires
and there make supplications to coyness,
singing songs of sacredness to forest flowers.

Let's love ourselves to stupor
and stoke the fires of fancies.

The Other Side of My Coin

That season of reveries is upon us,
to draw out her face from the well of desires.

Every closed eye uncovers
her smile, a maiden dancing in my head.

Her voice floats across my mind
like winds rejoicing at the arrival of rain;

so, I will dredge laughter from time past,
of the nights affections tricked sleep away.

And nights when the burning of passions
make fire blush with desire and envy,

nights when a hug was an eternity
of assurances to one drowning in despair.

The other side of my coin,
my fellow traveler of crossroads of twilight.

Adúmáradán

She of the delicate eyes
who decorates the chest with tingling nipples
that touch your lips and take you to heaven;
she who unwraps rhapsodies into melting kisses,
with eyes you can't resist calling your hands
into warmth and the aroma of a body's stories.

She who adorns the skin with unceasing shines,
whose blackness seals a lofty place in the pantheon
of unfading splendor, the beauty of perfect roundness
from the curves of delicate behinds.

Her love blossoms in my heart
despite the snow that covers the eye of sunlight.
Adúmáradán, abiding mate of the seasons of life,
she seizes upon my gaze, and desire burrows
into the dreams of an agile soul.

Overpowered. Pulsations, uncordial and fierce,
lead home to the waiting embrace of Anteros.
Adúmáradán, ebony queen of many graces,
lead me away to the land of requited magic.

This night is ours

to dream of the miracle
that enlivens the body;

blinded by love, we stagger
into each other, groans
dissolving into moans

intoxicated by the passions
of undulating thighs,
a weaver of dreams emerges

tales of arousals
tales of wetness, and of desires
in euphoria

bodies brush against each other
like the magic of engorged satiation
in the paradise
where beauties merge
into a chorus of roses.

It is the night of tricks
of coyness and the Coyote
and the ticks of flames;

Tonight, soft desires will stroke
the silky slopes of loins
and Èsù's erect man
will smile at us.

Letters to a Child

1

Dear Child,

I died yesterday.

But before my burial beckons,
These wailings and ramblings
Of House Members
Continue to torment me.

They say they will miss the Naira rain
At the bar just along the Villa.

They say the girls will forego
The night's customers
To show their last respect.

They even say they will be the first
To pour earth on my remains.

They say they will surely miss me
And my share of the national cake.

But I died, all the same.

2

Where is father to whisper madrigals
Into waiting ears, to unfurl flowers
That witness a season of fright?

Smiles glistening like grass-blades
garnished by the sun
May litter the playground,
But father says I mustn't go out.

In white Dansiki, flowing like a widow's tears,
He proudly demands that I stay indoors,
But I cannot ask a question—that will anger God.

Yet Tsunami calls . . .
I may survive.

She came before Ìwàlewà

Smiles that break dawn upon
us are rare, but not yours.
Let me down into their arms,
into plushness and the grace of my beloved.

And, today, Ìwàlewà, our fading tunes
will be heard again, back with rhythms
of growing intensities and shared breaths,

with you smiling again, and I flaunting my stein
to drink a fill of fresh orgies
as one out of the chamber of honey.

Echolalia

You, child, a beautiful character in the theatre of my dreams,
you plant sunflowers and sleepless nights in the garden
of prairie winters. And from your memories,
we pluck echoes of hopeful tomorrows,
LOLing lullabies to harvest your laughter.

You craft a mosaic of memories in my heart,
letting off babbles of blues in unending cuddles of blathers.
You splash smiles on my face and make me blush
like a first-time lover, each time you coo charm
from the vast empire of your mind.

And what are you thinking of again?
These tickles to your chin,
or the painting of blossoming flowers
hanging on the wall?

And the spittle from your suck this morning,
Was that your way of thanking mother for a feed?
Were your teethless smiles a chorus of generous adores?

What is the theme of your blank stare?
Are they unspoken gimmies you want seen?
Then let's pen prattles to them
and scribble sonnets for stuttering first steps,
or write verses to record innocence?

I shall be waiting here to read when
you write your poem for the empyreans ahead.

Where the Rivers Mix

Let's go to the place where the rivers mix.
We'll sit below the bridge and pretend
to fish from the waters before us.

"Aburo," I would ask, "do you see that salmon?"
An empty stare into space, with eyes
bulging like a bag of membranes
from the pregnancy of innocence.

You will sit with me, offering nothing by words,
only subdued laughter, and waiting
for a catch to paddle life into existence.

We sit and feel the breeze caress our skin,
while the currents of the waters pass by us,
without fish but dreams of sunshine
dancing upon our gaze.

III

Night of the Silent Drums

For Pius of Mellanby Hall, University of Ibadan

Shh! The mask has refused to dance tonight,
And the drums are hushed in bawling supplication to
Ogun's might.

Tap not your feet to the fading tunes of Gangan's splendor;
Night creeps in as the usual guest clad in sudden terror,

Calling us to a ritual of sighs and silences,
With hands folded upon thumping chests of death's tri-
umph.

Where are they whom we saw yesterday? We ask.
Shh! It is the night of the silent drums.

Wayfarer

Another Pius, of Isanlu

This final travel leads
to a home elsewhere, wearying innocence
with a flurry of thunderclaps
that scurry pain through tenderness,

through a heart harking
for father's return.
Words elude her,
eliding fears
and the agony that tears

without end.

A flight of stars on the wings of mourning;
meteoric, the descent of an unwanted morning:

and there he is, flying away from us,
crashing into the void that riddles the living.

In and out of our thoughts; never
to be touched again,
nor heard once more, he of the roaring laughter.

And there he is, flying away from her.
With reluctance, his back is turned
to those for whom his heart ached the most.

A lover's twilight.
A father's dusk,
heralding a cumulus of fears.

Ebbing.
receding,
the voices that once assured.

And as rest to the weary,
the wayfarer goes the way
of all flesh, to endless beginnings,

the primordial crossroads
of all branded pilgrims.

Death of an Unharried Poem

for Harry G.

There is a truth in every poem that ignites
a poem in every fire that burns with truth.

To write the ode of a man who crafted magic
so much its imperfections became
loathsome melodies in the music of his life
the warts and blemishes that sullied
the scarlet paper of nature's graces.

He fought hard to take it
but not here, for one soulless day
the curtains were drawn. With sunshine gone
his spirit soared to the ancestors
leaving behind the truths of his poems.

This gloomy trace of his rhymes,
can it capture the fractured sublimities of his life?

One Meets Two

1

We rescue beauty from your ashes today,
dust from the dust that never was,
smiling out tears to hide our fears.

We rescue beauty, and ourselves
from dreams and visions
of tiny footprints
that colour shadows, in the canvas of
lonely hearts.

One
meets
two,
and they
both forsake three;
mortals mounted by grief
for the pleasures of the Other.

As we lay wreaths to many absences,
we rescue you from the surreal gates
you almost entered, knowing
that your dwelling belongs elsewhere,
where guardian angels, wild with warmth,
giggle to your saintly souls
and whisper hope to us below.
That suffices us till you return.

2

They forged their communion
from memory, the breath of toil and blood,
with heaven's dew cascading upon them
where the sun sets hearts afire with hope.

And the two sail away across seasons,
to the full moons and symmetries of time
to meet from where they part:

In the belly of the country, twain as one,
she, with comely cheeks and he, keeper
of desires rupturing, to be born in paradise.

Theirs was not an attempt at life;
it was as made for two, locking horns gently
and fleeing away shadows and storms.

Like a glowing moon in the night skies,
they look back at the city they once loved,
and coiled into each other,
a retreat into daydreams at Eden's gates.

Ancestors

for Achebe and Madiba

One gleaned with tales and proverbs,
Mending history from the distortions
Of distractors
Masquerading as God's messenger.

The other called history
To a dialogue with conscience,
Fending boundaries
In the agora of truth
And forgiveness.

Metaphors burdened
With messages, for their voice.
Mantras brimmed with morals;
Both, freeing each other
From the shackles of the mind
And scaling walls
With the wisdom of words.

Two sides of a coin:
Each, an inscription of dreams
Fulfilled in the pages of freedom;
Each, seeking a Sahara of hope
And calling Beautiful Nubia
To a festival beyond self.

Elders transformed, a commune
Of watching ancestors, beholding
These *too* who light candles
To redeem the world.

Lord of the Crossroads

The paths tell stories of phallic dreams, tales
that scamper asunder at the crossroads of the first morn
—when uncertainty dripped in dribs and drabs,
frozen in the holy writs of a foreign god.

But Èsù battles their curse with silence,
tricking the ramblings of the fanatic's tongue,
with endless ayes to desires that are and knot.
Nowhere does laughter crackle more than
in the ignorance of Ifá's errand boy,
unknown by those whose voices call the most.

If by happenstance their slurs become calcified
in my visage, I have a cache of mischief
to bend their will to a brawl of night and day,
not with Hades' tantrums as though
a fit of rage converts the soul.

But as one kissing the earth
in a vague dream that swallows itself:
as a vision of swirling rhythms erupt
from the chthonian depth of your confusion,
it is I, òrìsà oríta, reclaiming my stories.

Mother Earth

Mother Earth is gold; her affections unfold
like a friend who never departs in the coming storms.
We cherish her grace and plough the face of her
that nurtures us through the race and plants
our feet in the tenderness of her strength.

Mother Earth is gold, golden is mother's love,
she who unfurls gems like scented flowers
for her children's desire to empower.
Your courage is the light that guides like
heaven's loving eye.

And the secret smiles of your tears
are music, the melodies that drive off fears.
Her prayers seal the future
and carry us through snowstorms and torture.

A poem for the earth is not forbidden.
We sing an Ode for her who defies odds,
for Mother who carries the destinies of others.
An Ode for you who hold us together.
For you, who bind our wounds and heal forever.

For you we sing, for you, we dance,
mother of gold, mother of all that's young and old.
For you, we sing an *Arioso,* for the land
to which we all return.

Móremí

Then, Èsù lived among men.
A two-eyed terror ruled the earth from the underworlds of Ife.
Only the brave could call him by his name: Dagború.

Móremí held the àrokò again to her startled face,
seeking to unloose its tongue, and pay homage to its pleas;
pleas for a noble heart to save these emissaries of sorrows.
She surrendered her necklace for the evening dance
and swiftly reached out for her special sword.

"Beware of his threats, my daughter," one of them said,
"the bites of his jaws and the fires from his mouth have taken many;
heed your heart's warnings: the danger he brings,
the seductions of his claws, and the grips of his embrace;
and here, tie this around your waist, may the gods be your guide."

And so Móremí plunged downward to meet Dagború,
she waited for him at the crossroads, his mischief to wrestle;
the path where ayé and ọrun watch mortals wrestle for vanities,
there she stood, breaking kolanuts for Ògún's favoured day.
"Dagború is finished," she said, stabbing the earth a second time.

The tremors brought him forth; he lurched out of darkness,
breathing hate and threats from scornful nostrils;
the abyss screeched with shrieks from Dagború's bragging chests.
He reached out to Móremí's prattling feet, lifting her off the ground.
Gbòsà! Her back kisses the earth in pain. Dagború roared!

And as he bent to tear bloodied hands into her neck,
Mórẹmí jerked out of sleep and planted a dagger into Dagború;
a monstrous cry and his weight cusped to a crash.
Mórẹmí staggered back into her deathly sleep until he
who had delighted himself with the fight brought her a drink.

The people danced to the songs of her return that night.
Men and music spoke of her fame,
princes desired her beauty and bravery;
"Mórẹmí's name will live forever in our hearts,
and this land shall always be yours to rule," they told her.

During the days Èsù lived among men,
a two-eyed terror ruled the earth from the underworlds of Ife.
Only the brave could call him by his name: Dagború.
Only Mórẹmí, a princess of Ifẹ̀, could deliver the land.

ACKNOWLEDGEMENTS

Profound thanks to Razak Malik and Gbenga Adeoba who both first compiled and edited some of the earliest versions of many poems in this collection. Also, Andréa Ledding, Peter Akinlabi, Tade Ipadeola, Jumoke Verissimo, Gbeminyi Adekanbi, and Servio Gbadamosi—I salute you all for reading, and offering invaluable suggestions. Also, I am grateful to Professors Remi Raji, Ignacio Carvajal, and Nduka Otiono for their help with the collection. Thanks for the blurbs, and foreword, respectively. Finally, to Mawenzi House Publishers. Thank you for your amazing work on this project. Nothing stays forever broken when a mender's kindness is uncracked.

JAMES YEKU is a Nigerian-Canadian writer who lived in Saskatoon for six years before moving to Lawrence, Kansas, where he is an Assistant Professor of African Digital Humanities at the University of Kansas. He teaches introductory courses in African studies, Black masculinities, and digital literary studies. Yeku's poetry and fiction have been recognized with awards and nominations, including the University of Ibadan Okigbo Poetry Prize in 2008 (First runner-up).

"Although the politics of my Nigerian homeland animate several of the poems, their most abiding rumination is on the poetic space in which I have attempted to enunciate the constancy of change and the disruption of fixities. The intersections of the human experiences become evident in poems that make legible how enduring the harsh realities of winter storms and frost bites remind me of the adversities of home that so traumatize you that you feel the best gestures of love must be from afar."